Famous & Fun Pop Christmas

10 Appealing Piano Arrangements

Carol Matz

Famous & Fun Pop Christmas, Book 3, contains popular Christmas-season favorites, many originally from movies, radio and television. The arrangements can be used as a supplement to any method. Simple eighth-note rhythms are used, but dotted-quarter notes are avoided. Several arrangements are written with one sharp or flat in the key signature. The optional duet parts for teacher or parent add to the fun. Enjoy playing these well-loved Christmas favorites!

Carol Matz

Produced by
Alfred Music Publishing Co., Inc.
P.O. Box 10003
Van Nuys, CA 91410-0003
alfred.com

Printed in USA.

ISBN-10: 0-7390-8292-2
ISBN-13: 978-0-7390-8292-8

Frosty the Snowman

Words and Music by
Steve Nelson and Jack Rollins
Arranged by Carol Matz

Moderately

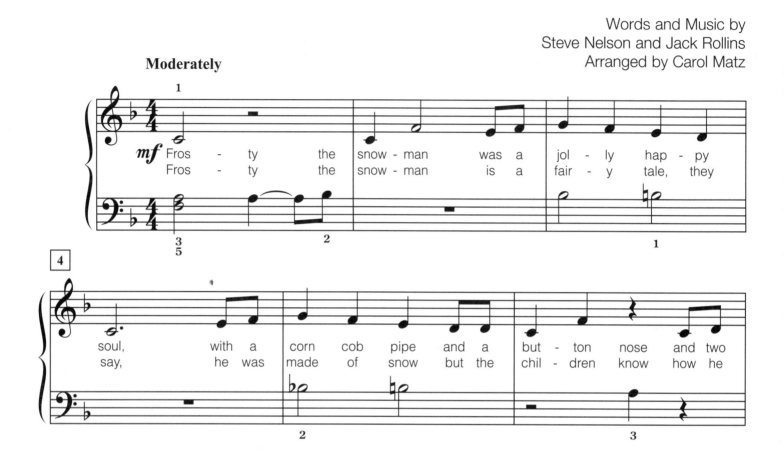

Fros - ty the snow - man was a jol - ly hap - py
Fros - ty the snow - man is a fair - y tale, they

soul, with a corn cob pipe and a but - ton nose and two
say, he was made of snow but the chil - dren know how he

DUET PART (Student plays one octave higher)

Moderately

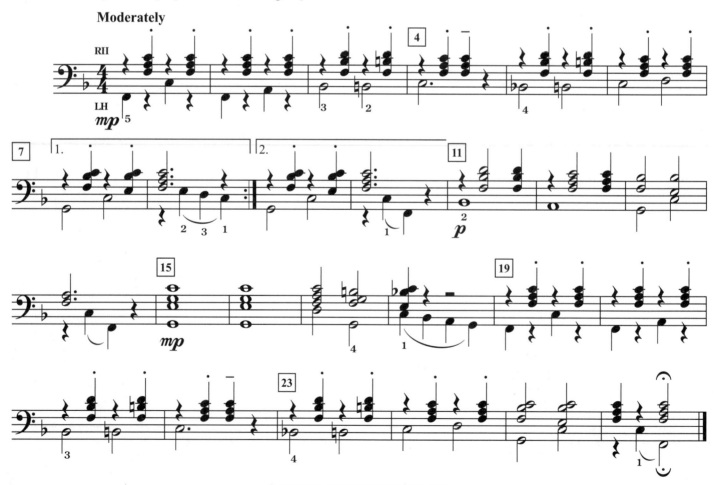

Santa Claus Is Comin' to Town

Words by Haven Gillespie
Music by J. Fred Coots
Arranged by Carol Matz

Moderately

You better watch out, you better not cry,
making a list, you and checking it twice,

better not pout, I'm telling you why:
gon-na find out who's naught-y and nice.
San - ta Claus is com - in' to

DUET PART (Student plays one octave higher)

Moderately

RH

LH

Let It Snow! Let It Snow! Let It Snow!

Words by Sammy Cahn
Music by Jule Styne
Arranged by Carol Matz

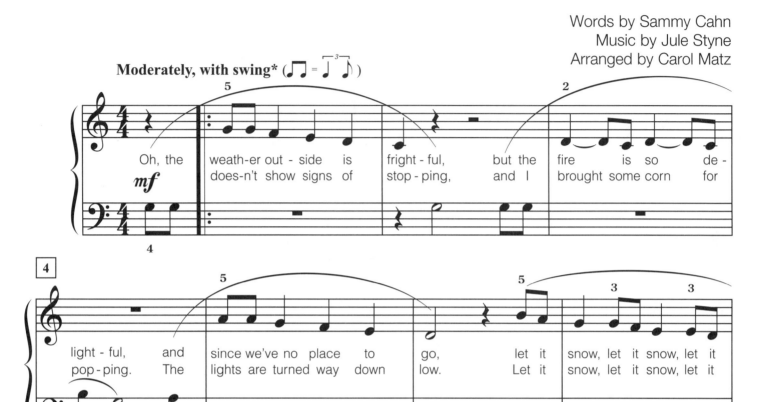

Oh, the weath-er out-side is fright-ful, but the fire is so de-
doesn't show signs of stop-ping, and I brought some corn for

light-ful, and since we've no place to go, let it snow, let it snow, let it
pop-ping. The lights are turned way down low. Let it snow, let it snow, let it

* Play all eighth notes with an uneven, long-short pattern.

DUET PART (Student plays one octave higher)

The Little Drummer Boy

Words and Music by
Harry Simeone, Henry Onorati and Katherine Davis
Arranged by Carol Matz

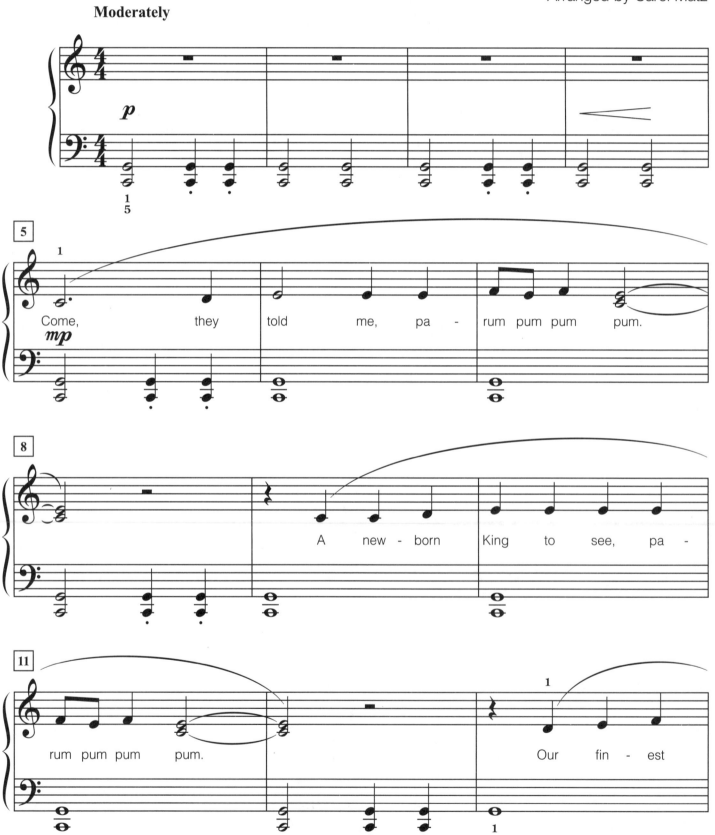

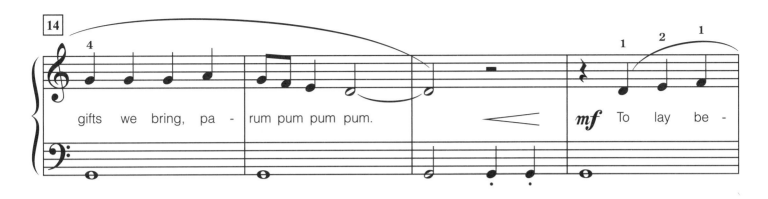

gifts we bring, pa - rum pum pum pum. *mf* To lay be -

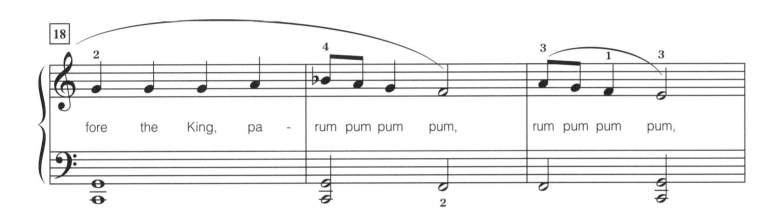

fore the King, pa - rum pum pum pum, rum pum pum pum,

rum pum pum pum. So to hon - or Him, pa - *mp*

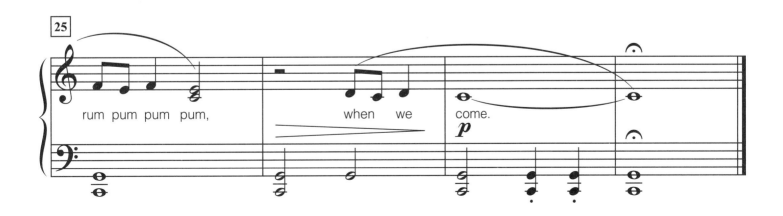

rum pum pum pum, when we come. *p*

Sleigh Ride

Music by Leroy Anderson
Words by Mitchell Parish
Arranged by Carol Matz

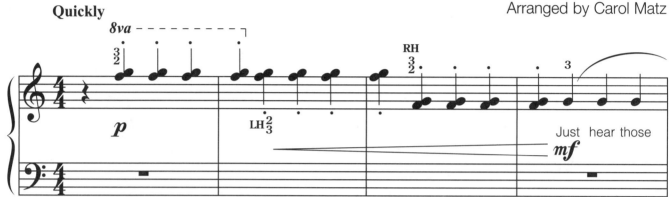

Just hear those

DUET PART (Student plays one octave higher)

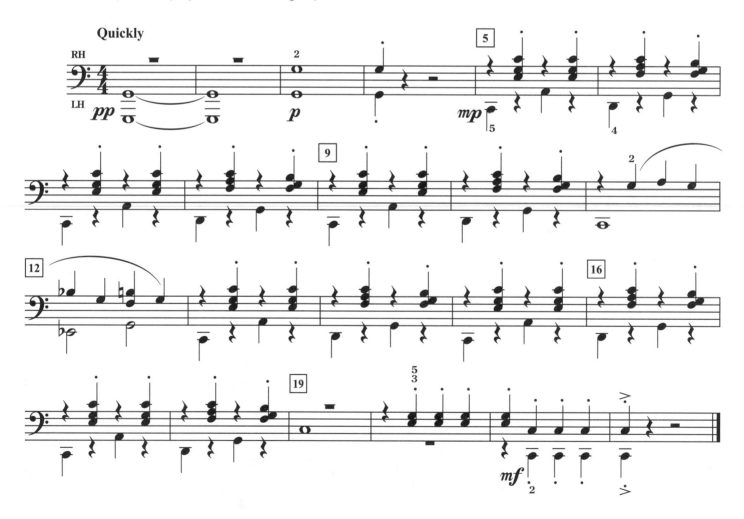

Ding, Dong, Merrily on High

Traditional
Arranged by Carol Matz

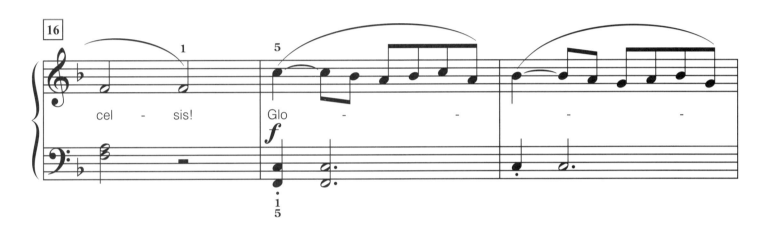

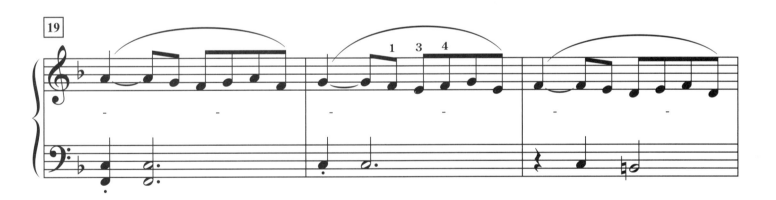

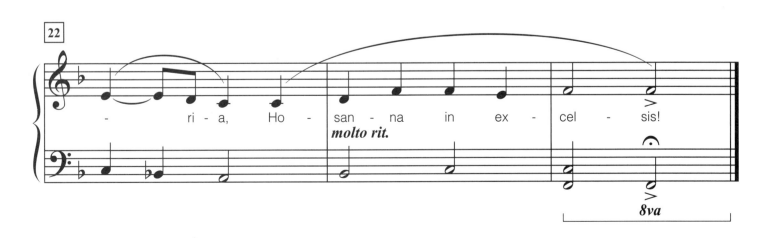

Ukranian Bell Carol

Traditional
Arranged by Carol Matz

Moderately fast

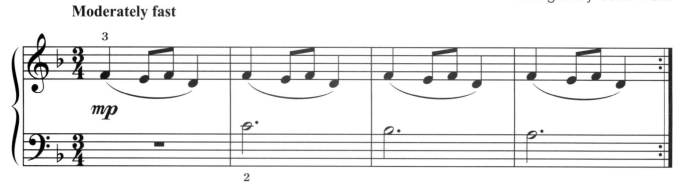

DUET PART (Student plays one octave higher)

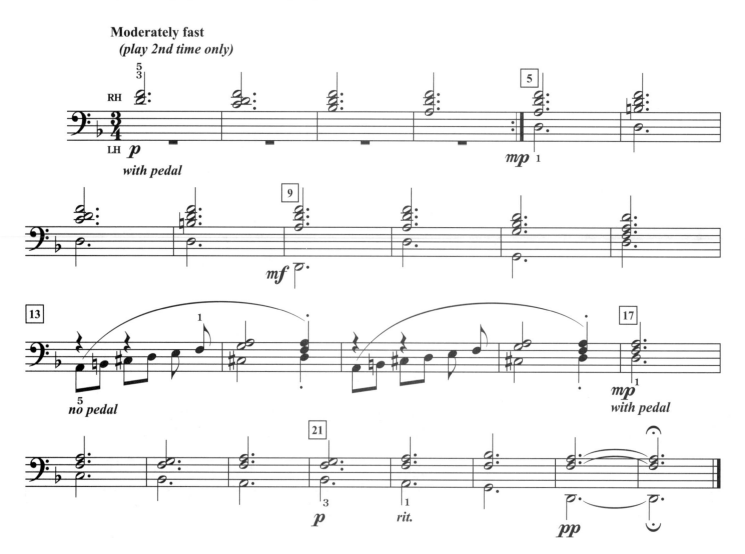

15

(no pedal with duet)

March

(from *The Nutcracker*)

By Peter Ilyich Tchaikovsky
Arranged by Carol Matz

* *Play eighth notes with an uneven, long-short pattern.*

DUET PART (Student plays one octave higher)

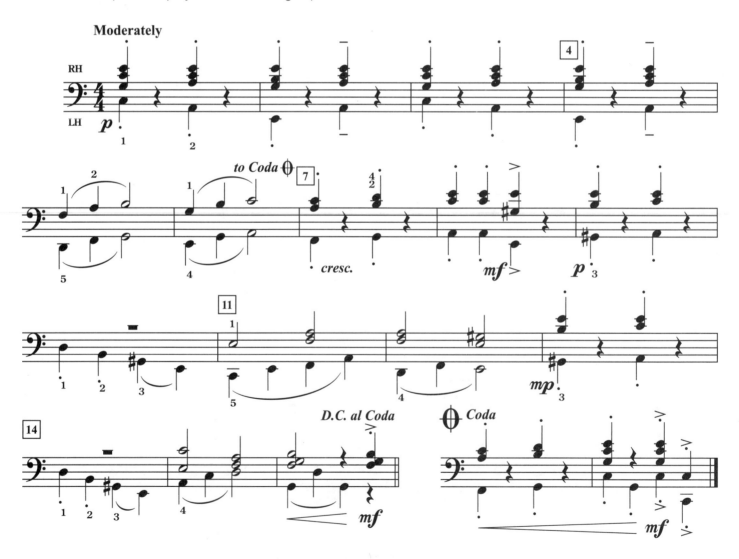

Jingle Bell Rock

Words and Music by
Joe Beal and Jim Boothe
Arranged by Carol Matz

* *Play all eighth notes with an uneven, long-short pattern.*

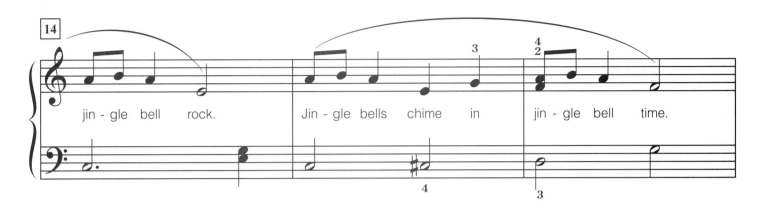

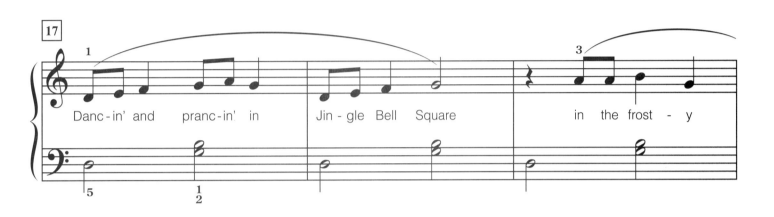

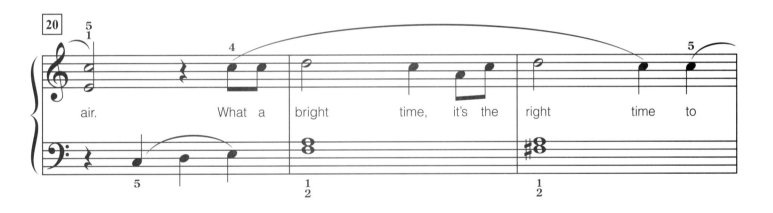

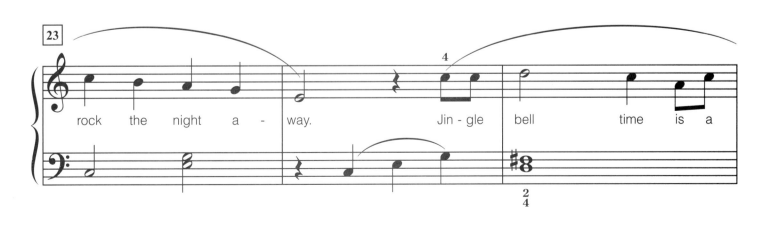

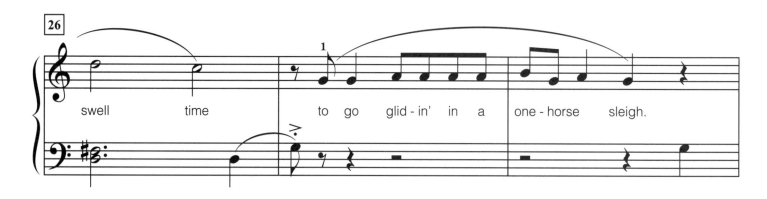

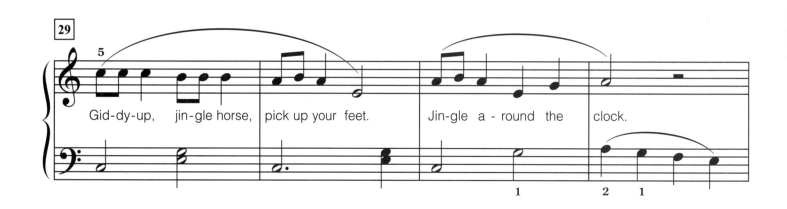

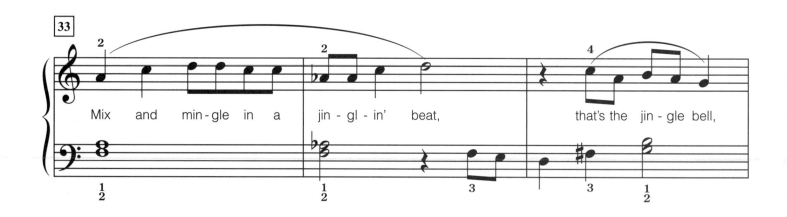

Feliz Navidad

Words and Music by José Feliciano
Arranged by Carol Matz

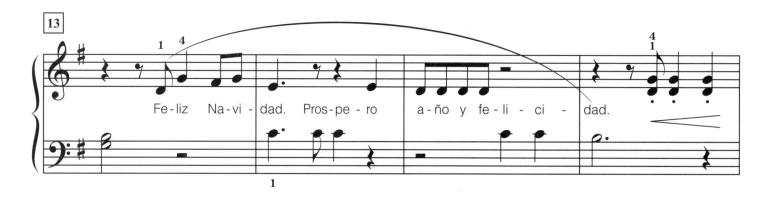

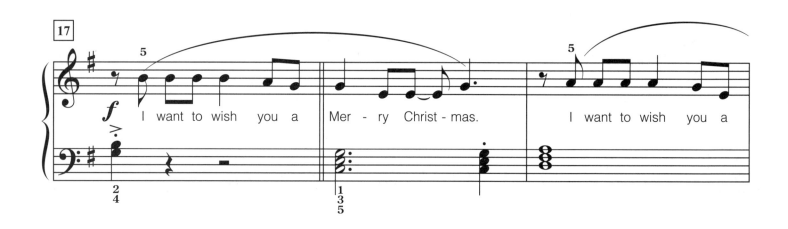

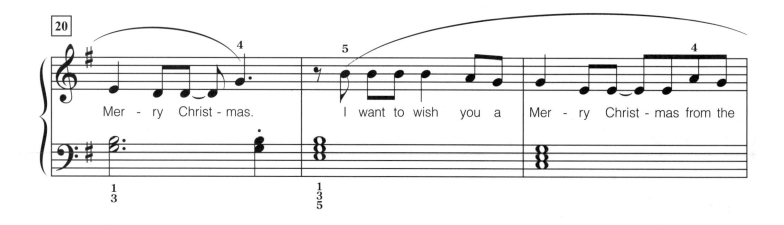

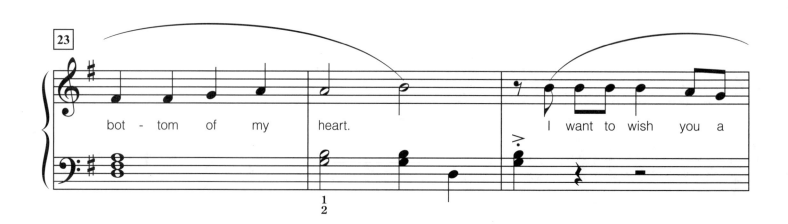